Kinky Bondage Sex Coupons

BY: RYAN HOTH

ISBN:10: 1533596611
ISBN-13: 978-1533596611

Tear Out The Coupons To Redeem

This Sex Coupon is for you to tie me up, blindfold me, and use a vibrating dildo on me until I orgasm 3 times.

After I will reward you with a blowjob wearing whatever you want me to wear.

Back Side Of
Coupon

This sex coupon is for you to spank me, while I pleasure myself to orgasm.

Back Side Of Coupon

This sex coupon is for you to bend me over a table and lick and suck me from anus to pussy, while I hold a vibrator to my clitoris.

As a reward I will suck on your balls, while using my hand to jack you off.

Back Side Of
Coupon

This sex coupon is for you to be my sex slave for a day. You must do whatever I say and want. If I want a massage, I get it. If I want oral I get it. Anything I want I get.

As a reward I have to be your sex slave for a day.

Back Side Of Coupon

This sex coupon is for you to write down 3 fantasies and tonight we will do one of them. The next two will follow during the week.

Back Side Of Coupon

This sex coupon is for you to hold my arms above my head and fuck me fast and hard.

Fuck me good and as a reward I will let you do it to me.

Back Side Of
Coupon

This sex coupon is for you to tie me down spread eagle to a bed, blindfold me and put ear phones in my ears with music. Then you must flog me and pleasure me orally for an hour.

Back Side Of Coupon

This sex coupon is for you to slap my ass and fuck me doggystyle. Stick a thumb and my butt and massage it, while you Fuck Me

Back Side Of Coupon

This sex coupon is for you to try anal training. Using a small anal vibrator place it in my ass and the lick and suck my clitoris.

As I reward I will strip dance for you

Back Side Of Coupon

This sex coupon is for you to give me a blowjob, while holding a vibrater bullet between my balls and anus.

As a reward I will fuck you and hold a vibrator on your clit

Back Side Of
Coupon

This sex coupon is for you to 69 with me.

Whoever orgasms first has to orgasm two more times before 69 ends.

Have Fun.

Back Side Of
Coupon

Tie me to a chair and pleasure me orally. Then switch. Who ever gets the other one off the fastest doesn't have to be spanked 50 times.

Back Side Of Coupon